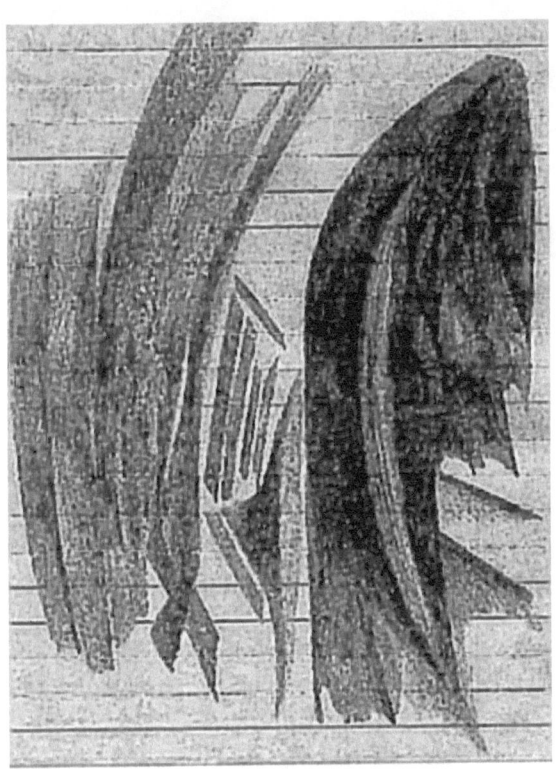

Cut For The Seas

<u>Welcome</u>

This is the fourth book of artwork in the Surreal Dream series. I hope you will find something to inspire your imagination here, perhaps to dream they say. If you are a lover of art then you might find this collection interesting. As I have said in one of the previous volumns some of the inspiration is taken from forign films (AMC Classics) and the rest from dreams, imaginings and pure muse. The images presented are compilations of many things. A good piece of art is something you can look at twice or multiple times and see something new at each turn.

Hopefully you will be entertained. So…….on with
the show.

Ron Koppelberger Jan. 2013

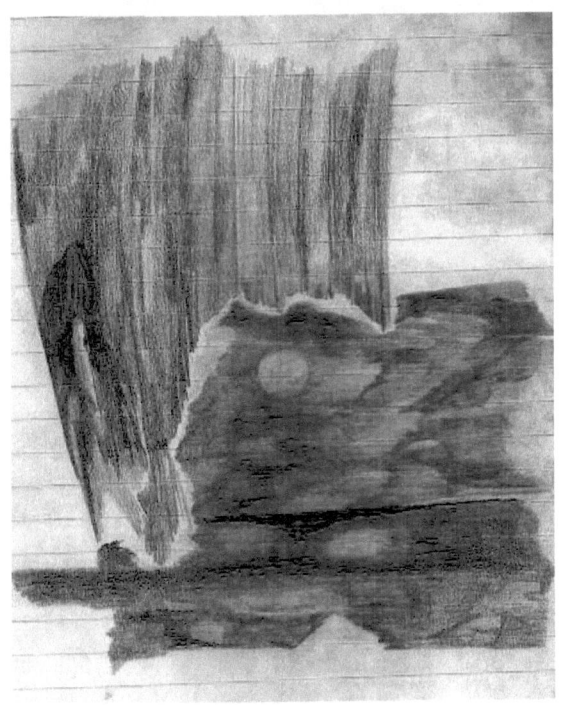

The Moons Reflection

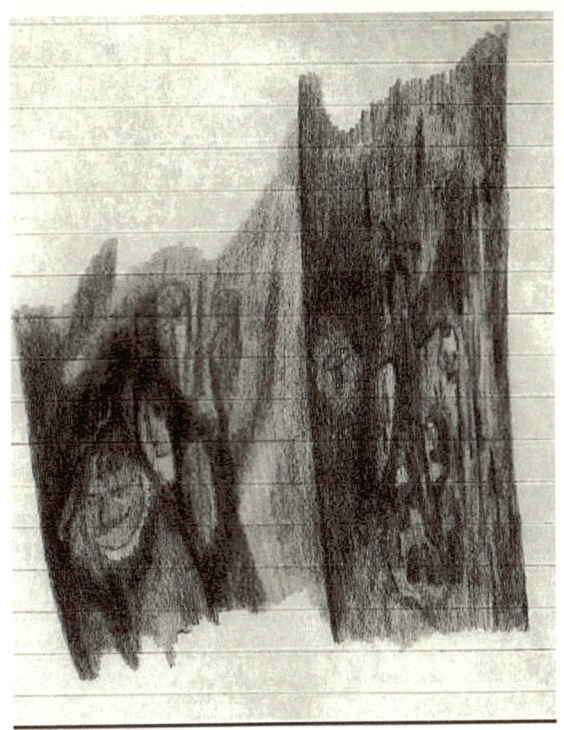

Regal Reflections

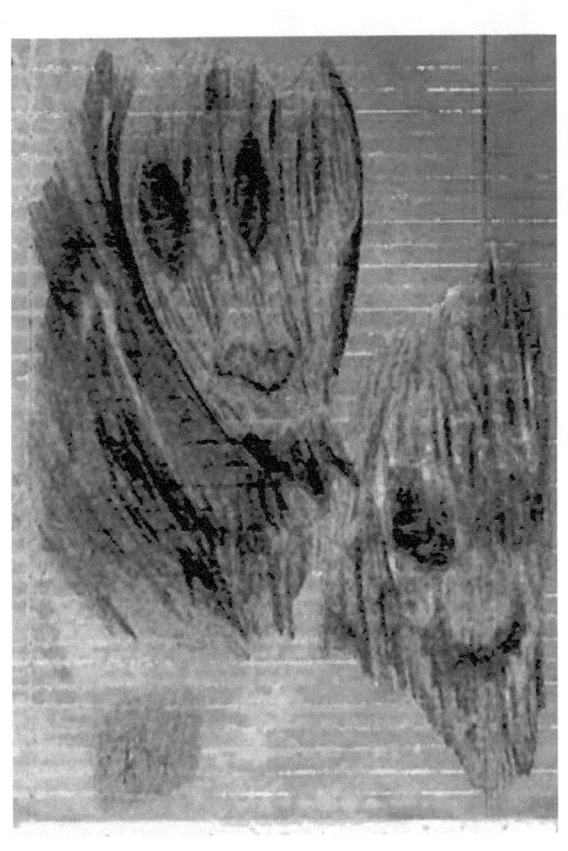

Hidden Secrets of Appearance

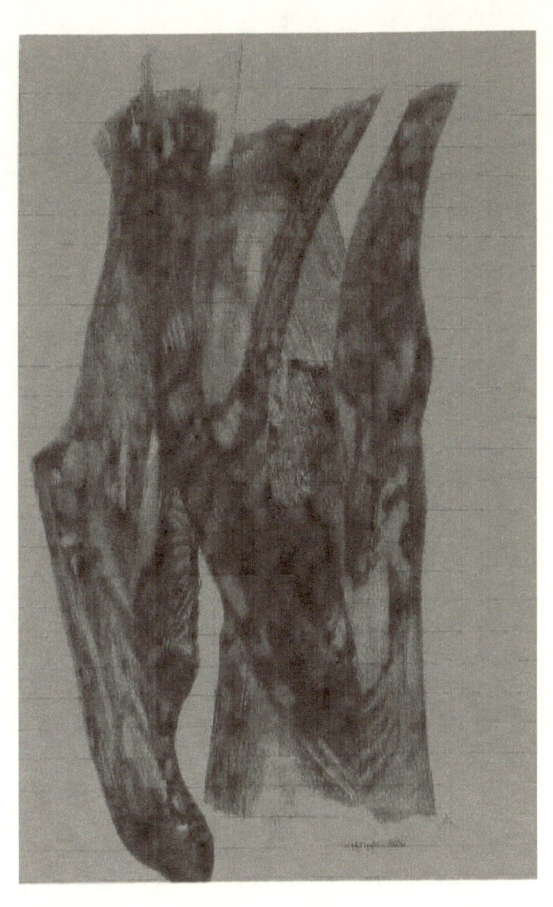

Butterfly In Red

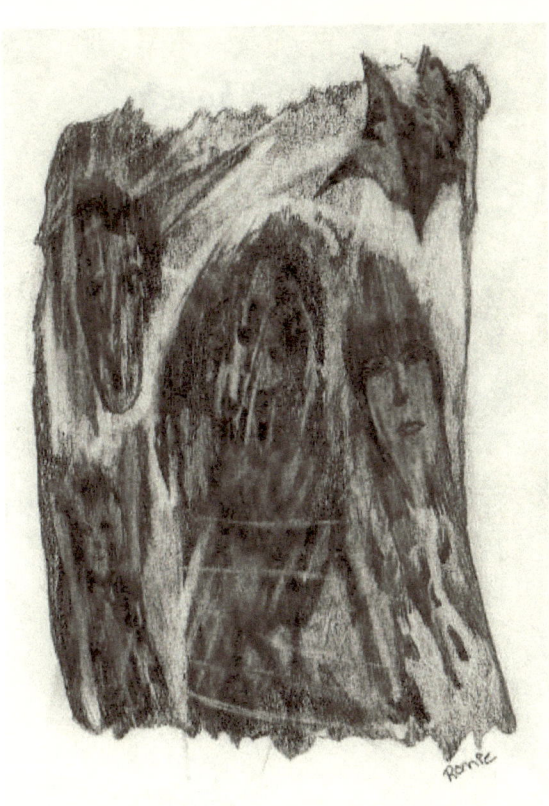

Her Crazy Thought

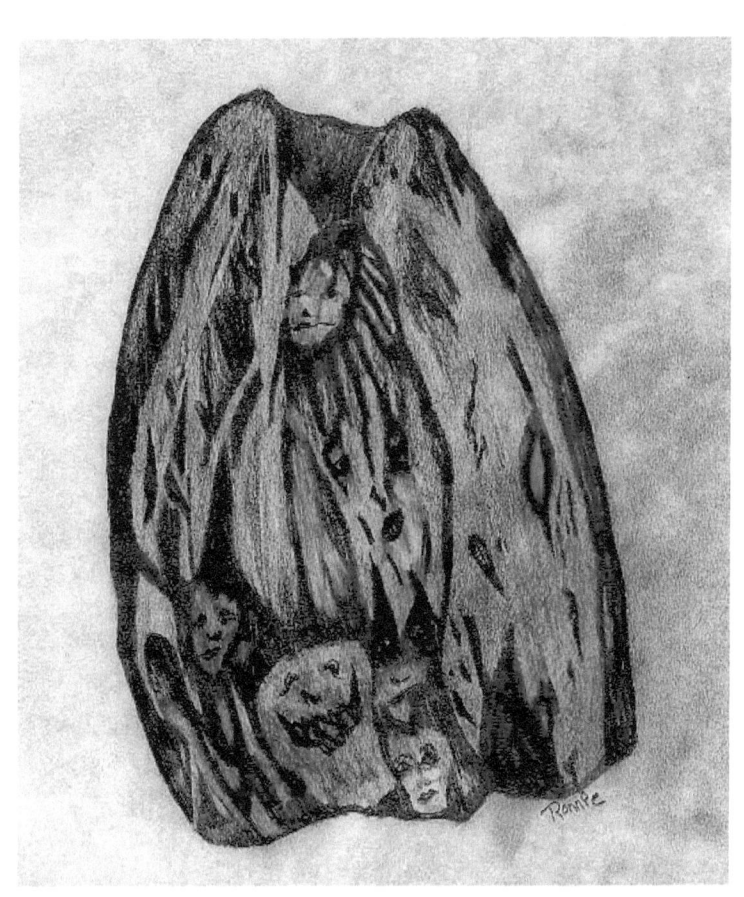

Sun Goddess

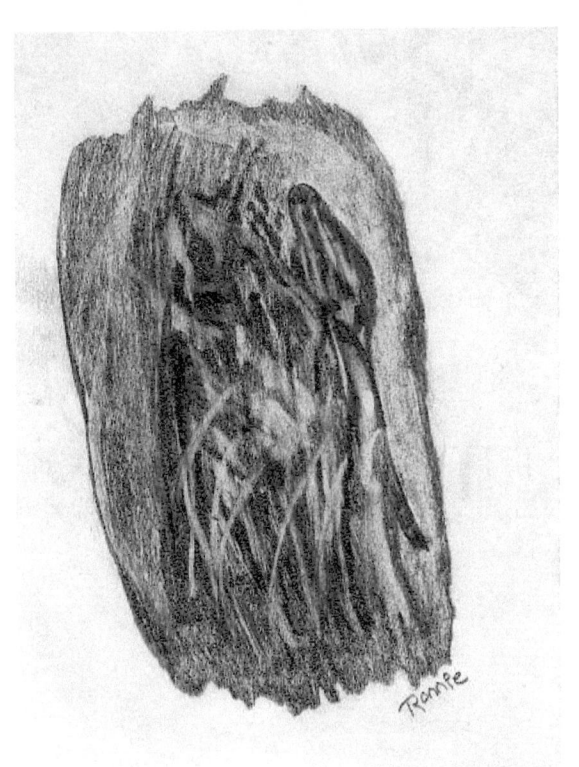

The Woman and the Crow

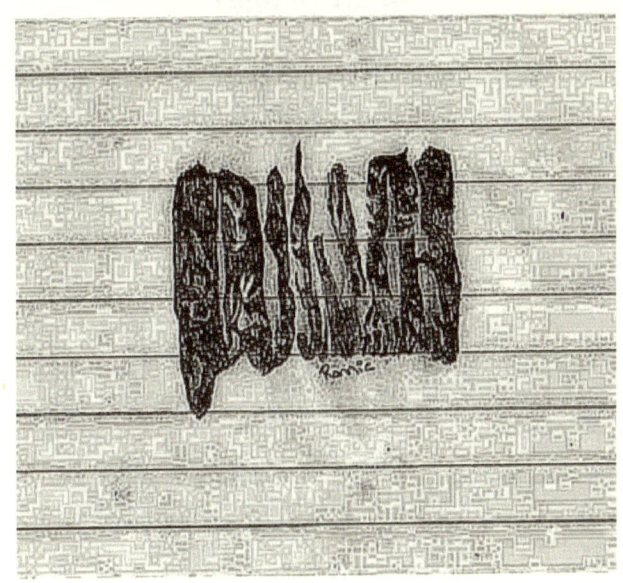

Small Images

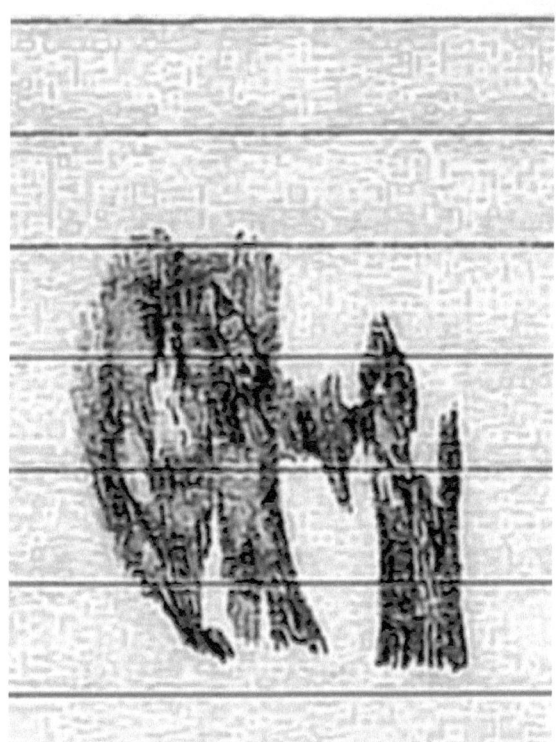

Royal Parade

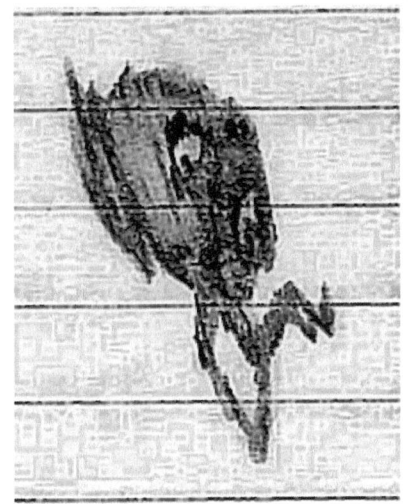

The Swing

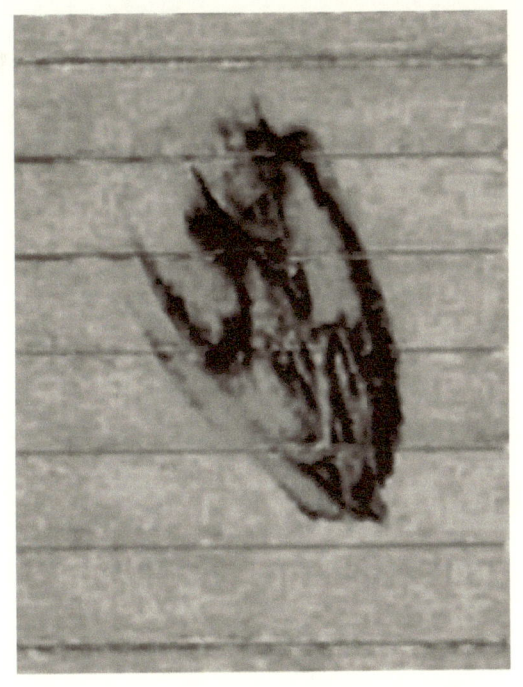

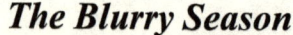

The Blurry Season

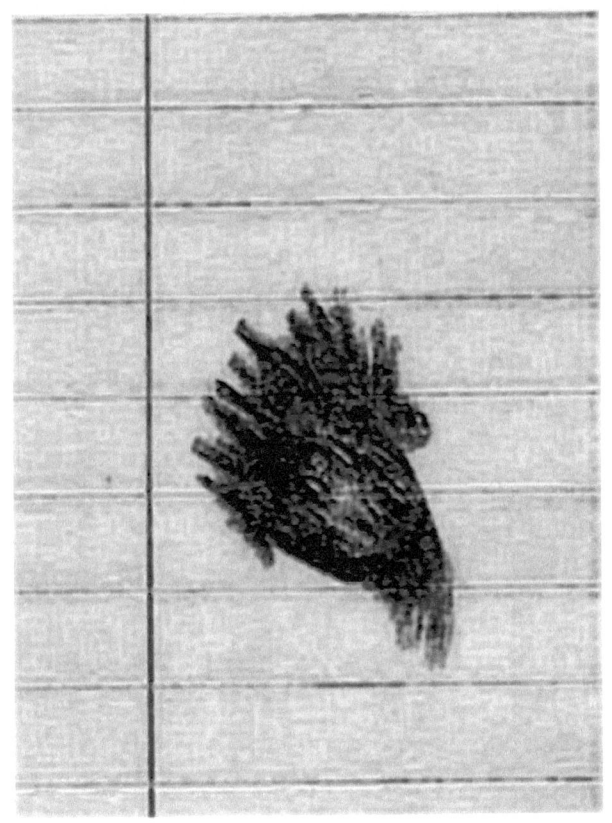

The Wanderer

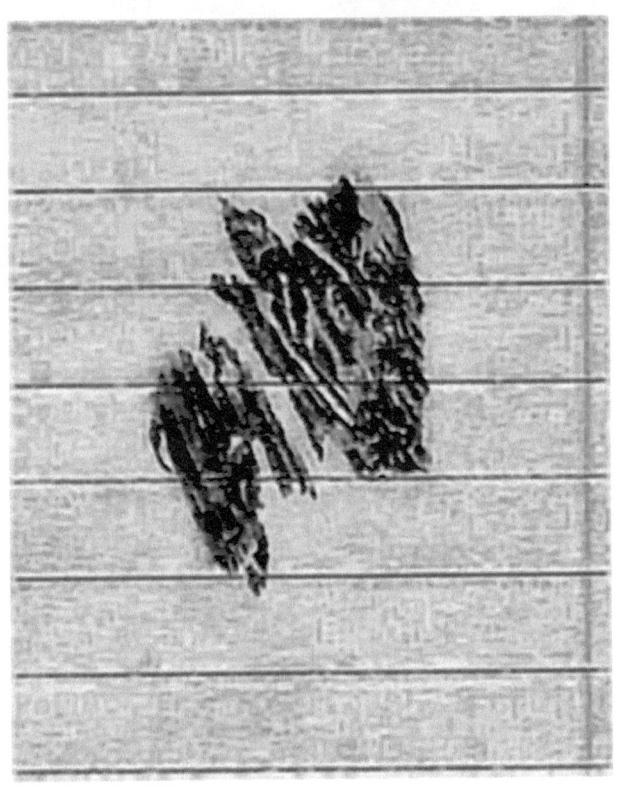

Jumbled Mirage

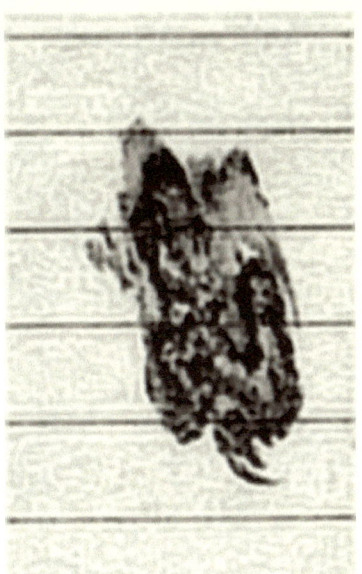

Man In Mystery

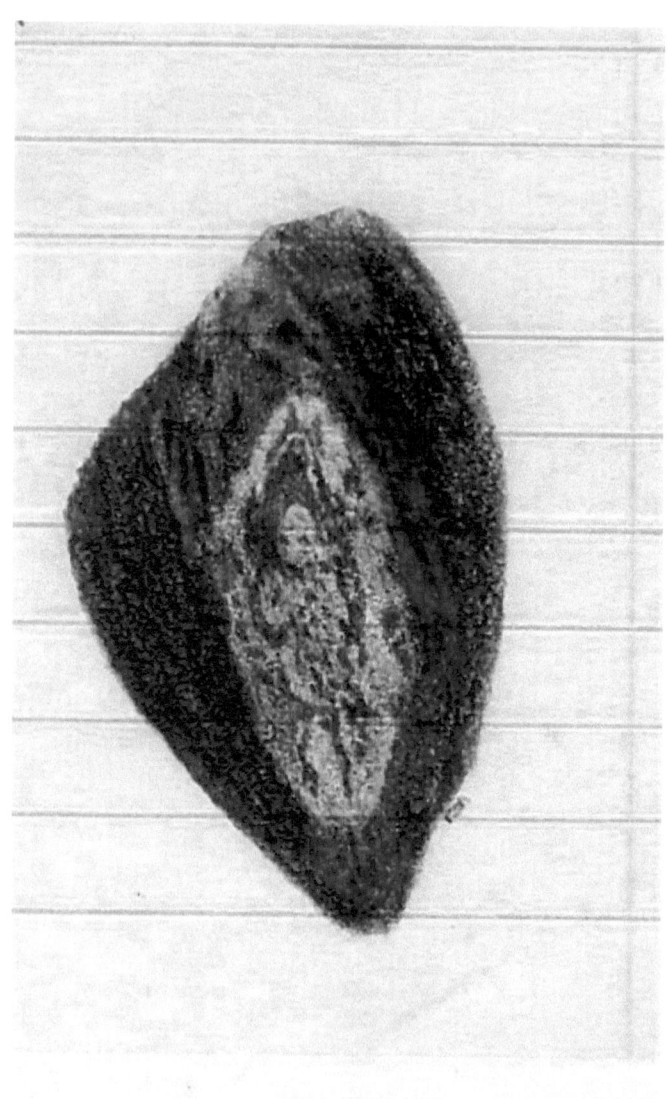

Hiding In Secret

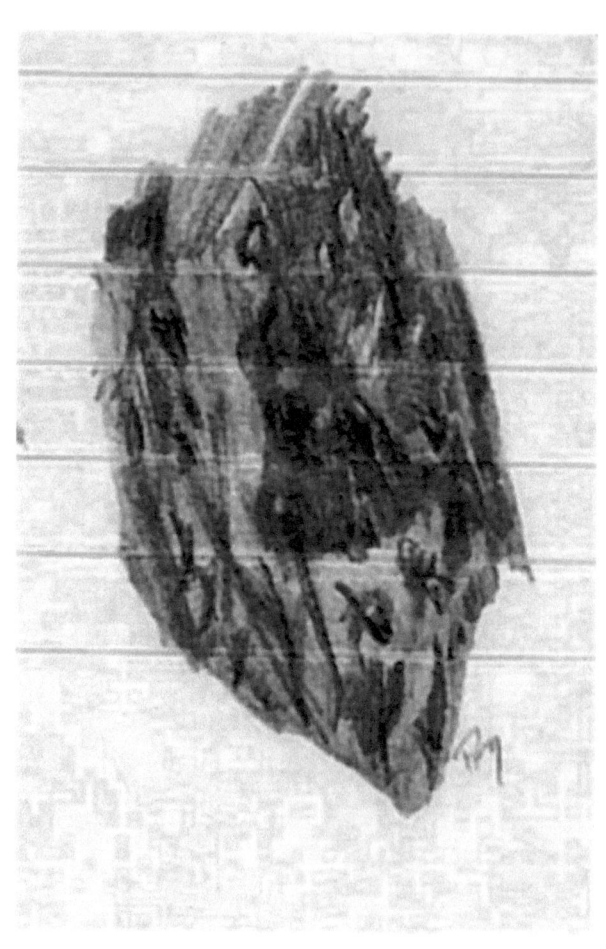

Royal Walk

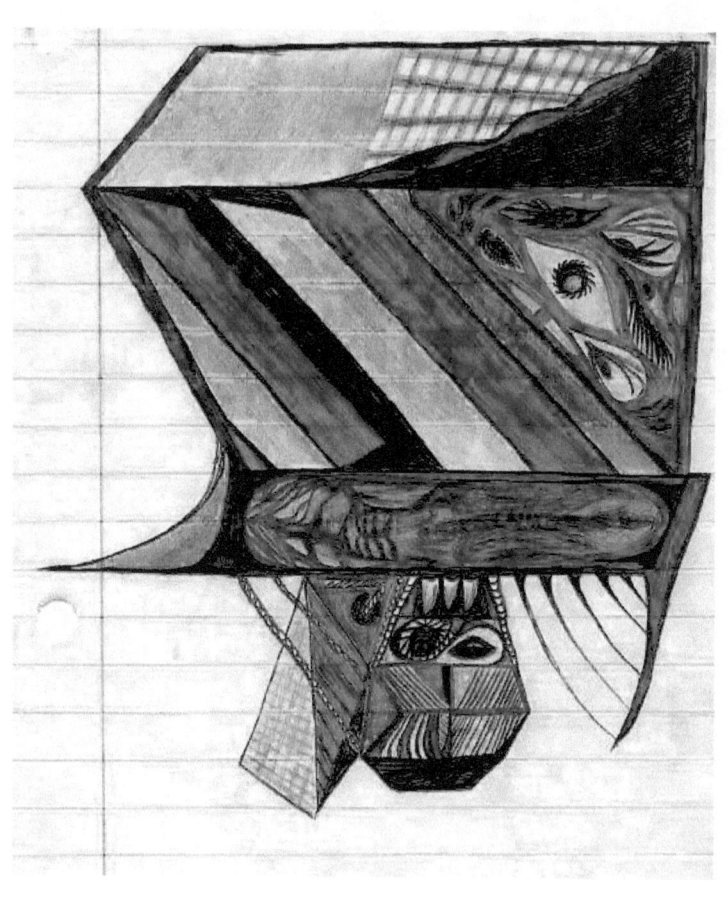

Mirrors

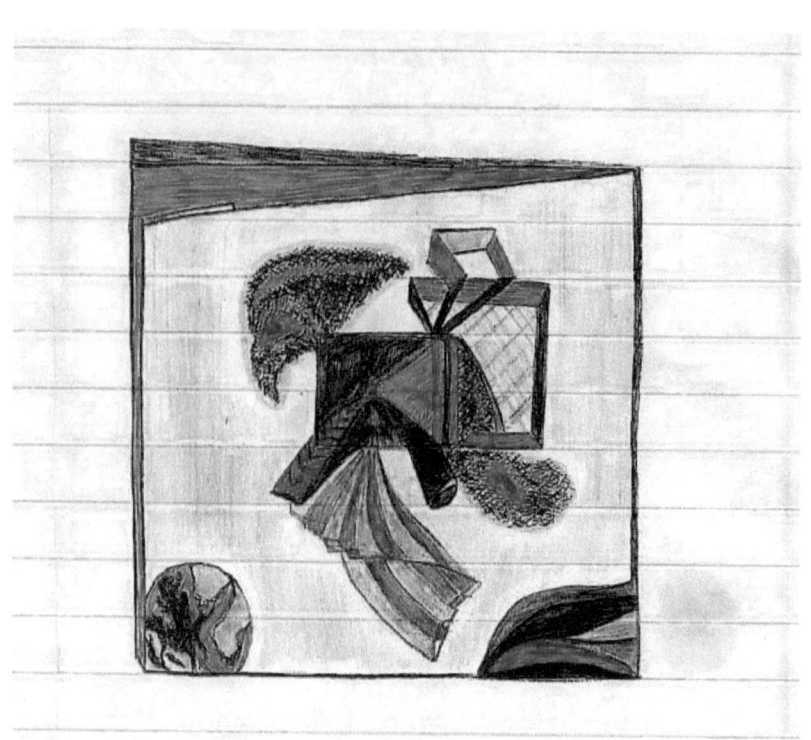

The Cube

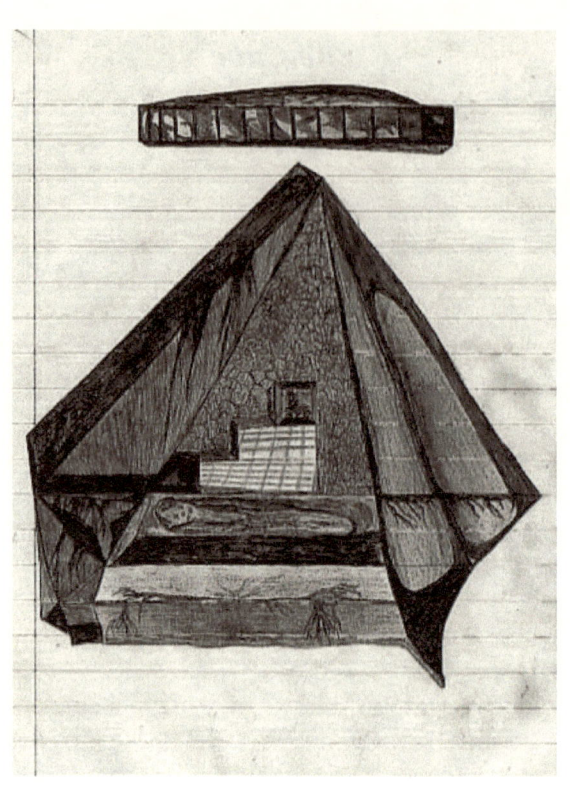

The Burial

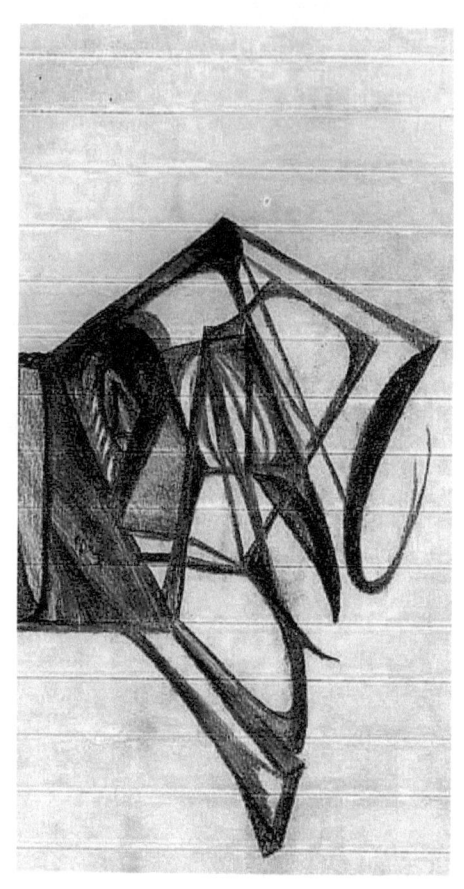

Angles Unfolding

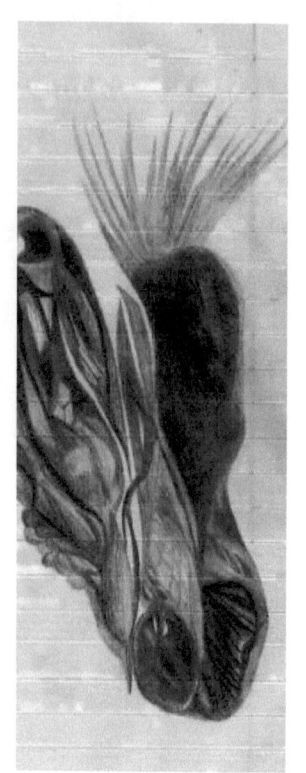

A Tuft of Crabgrass

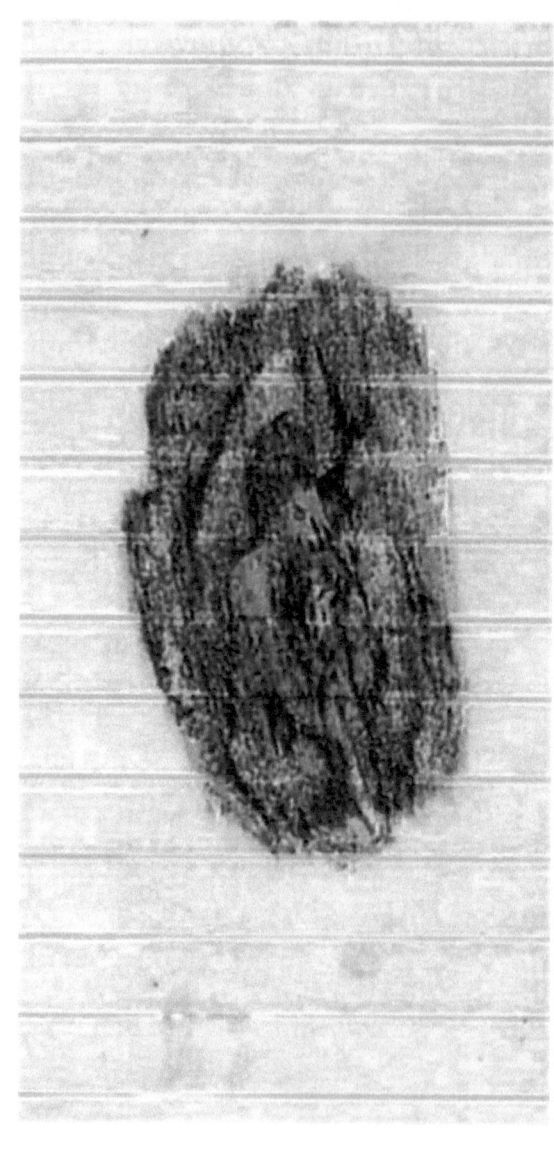

Mother and Daughter

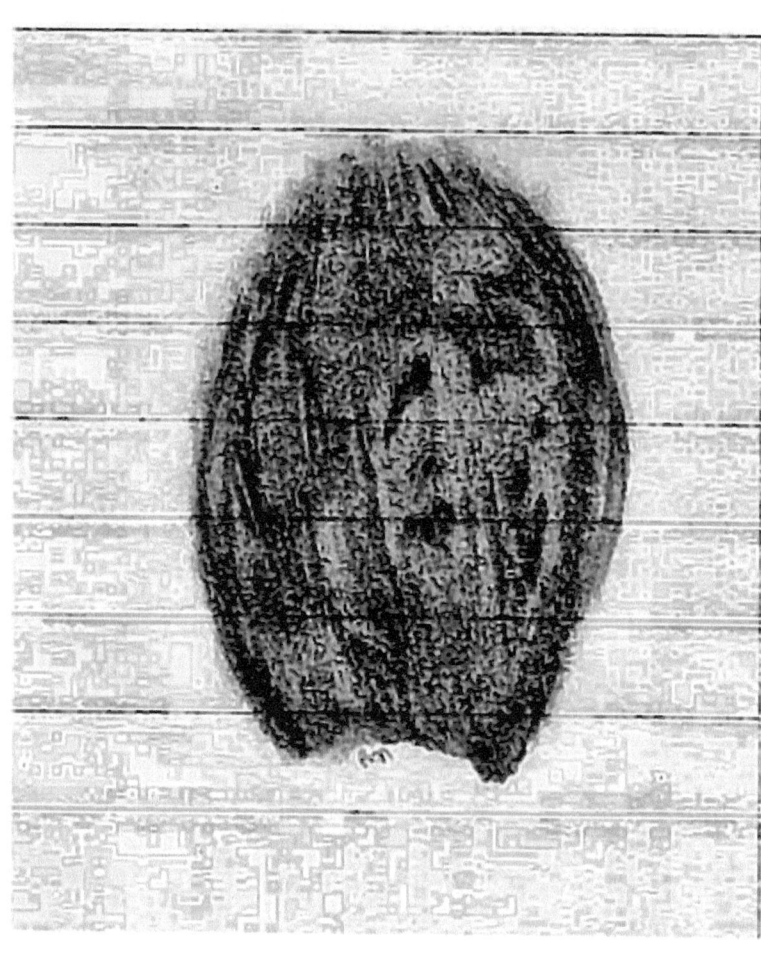

Horns

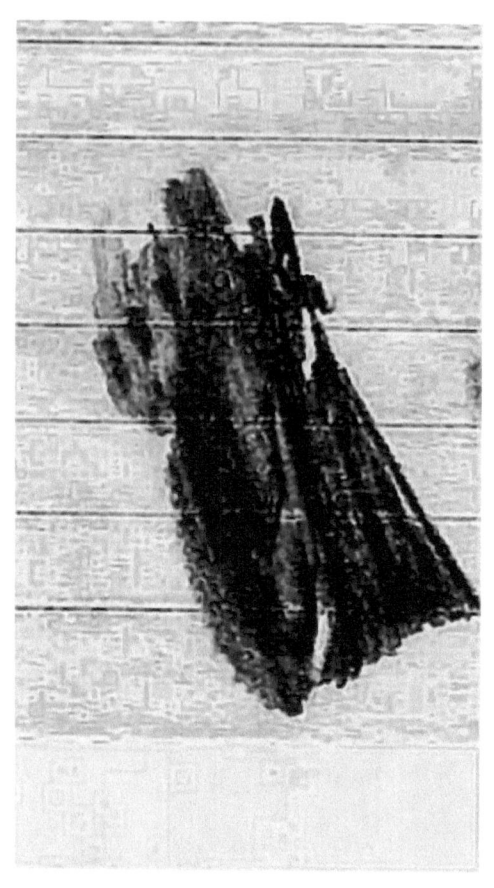

Standing Tall

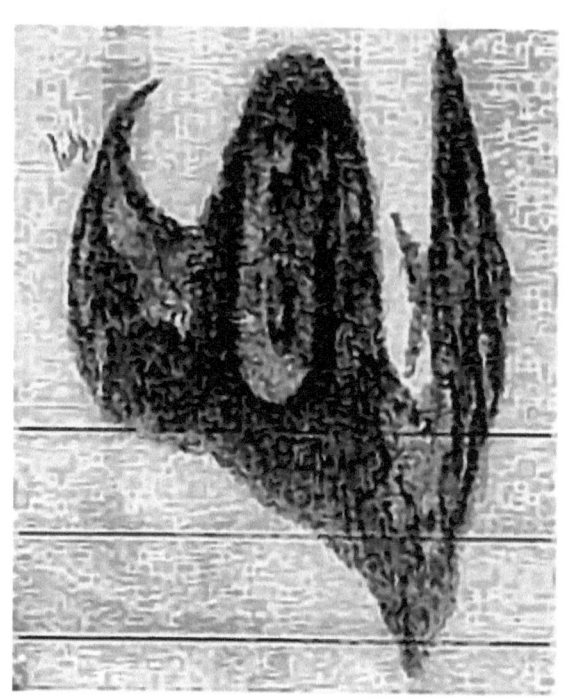

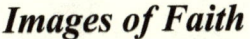

Images of Faith

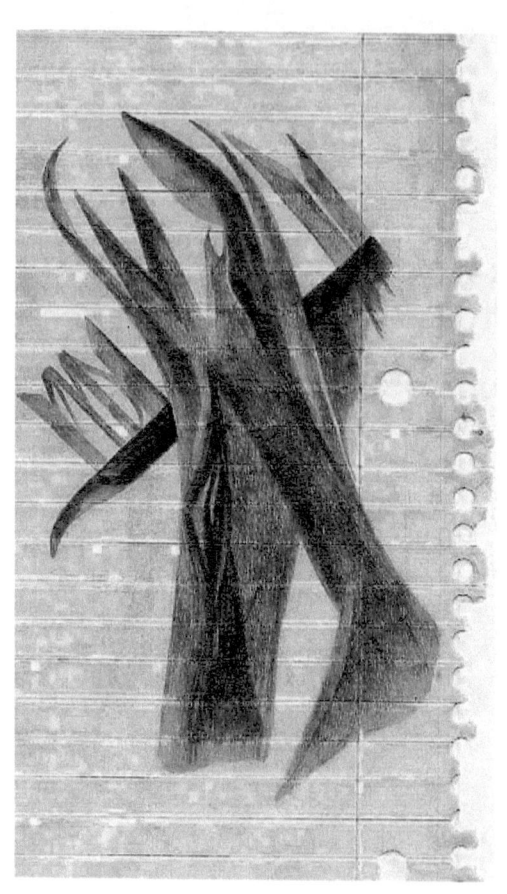

Images in Gray

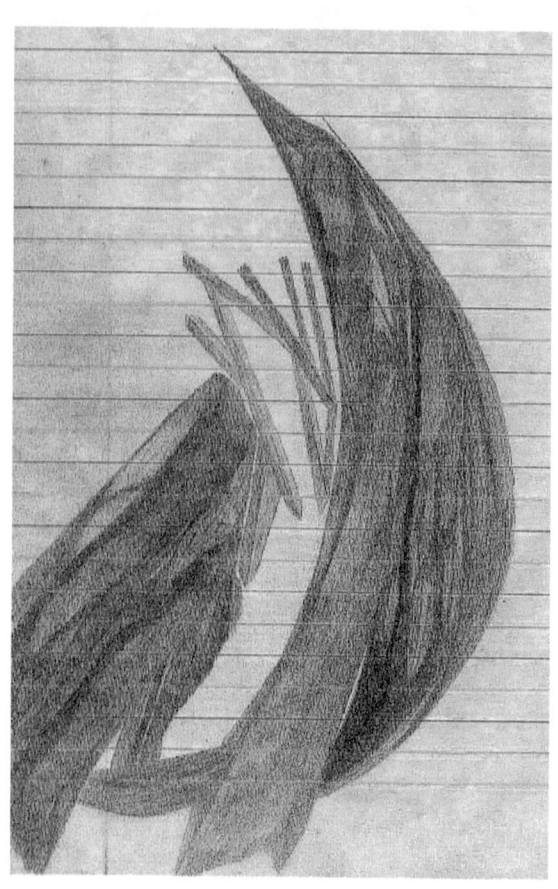

Cresent Moon

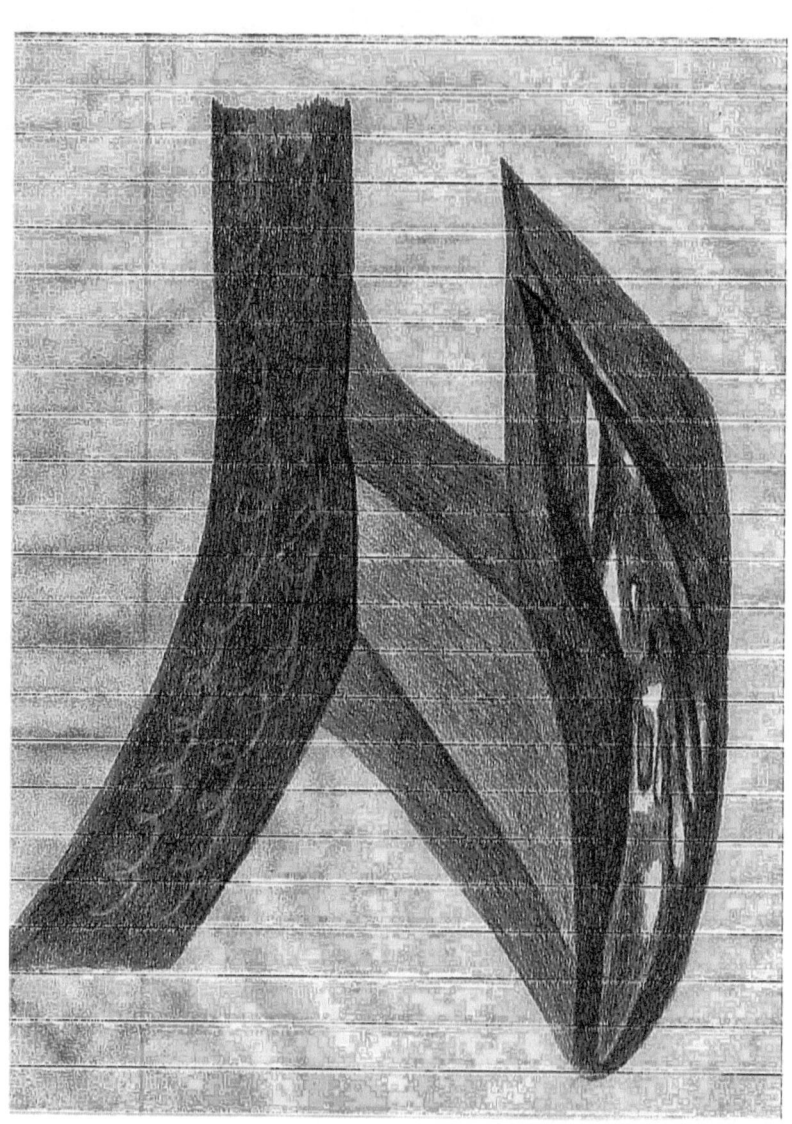

Fear In Steps

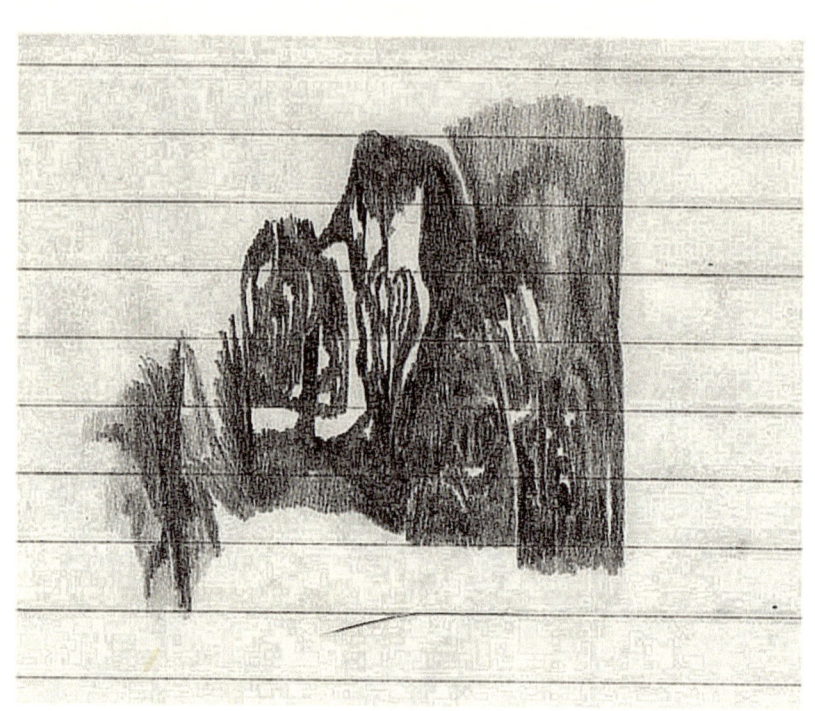

A Reflection Of Sanity

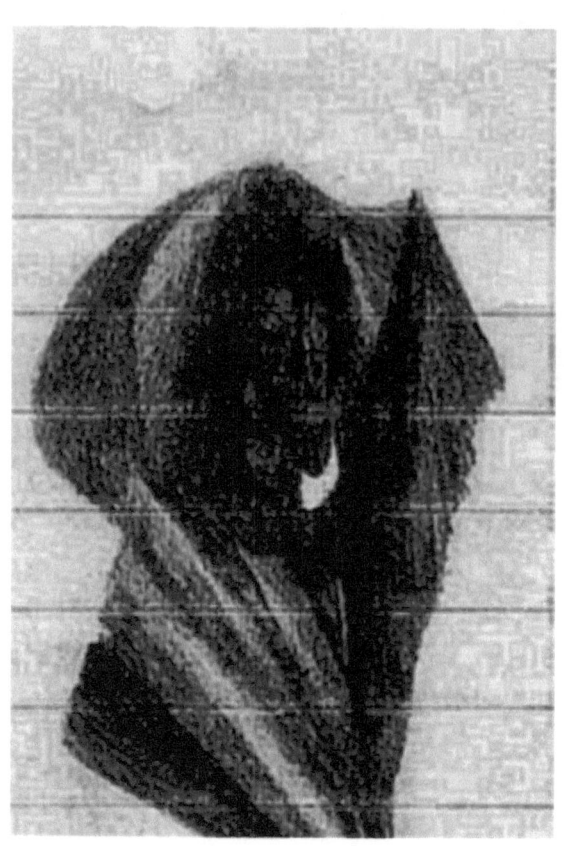

Arrayed

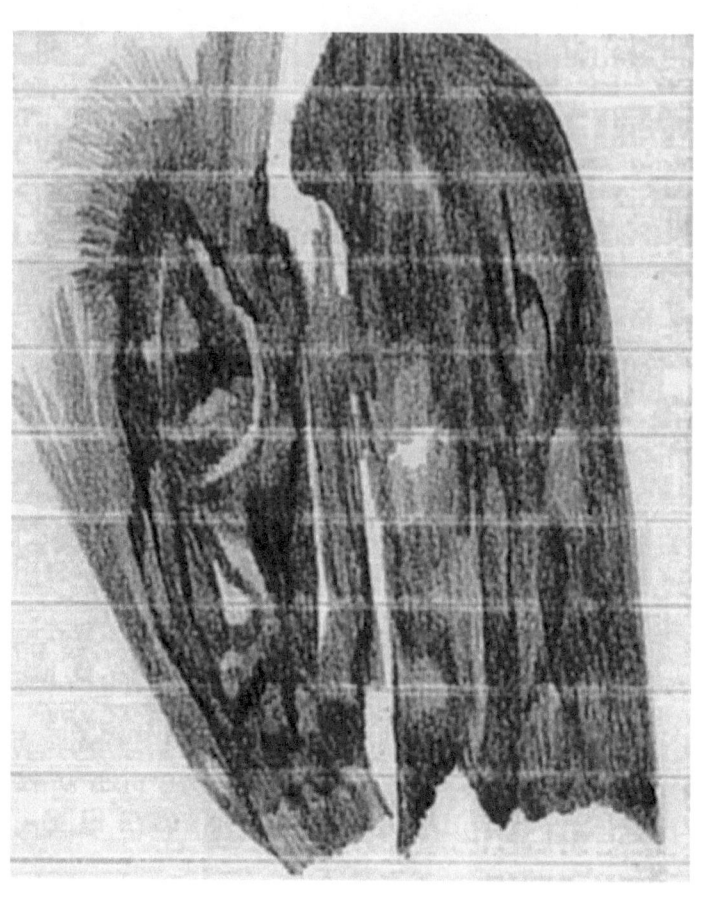

Monsters Among Us

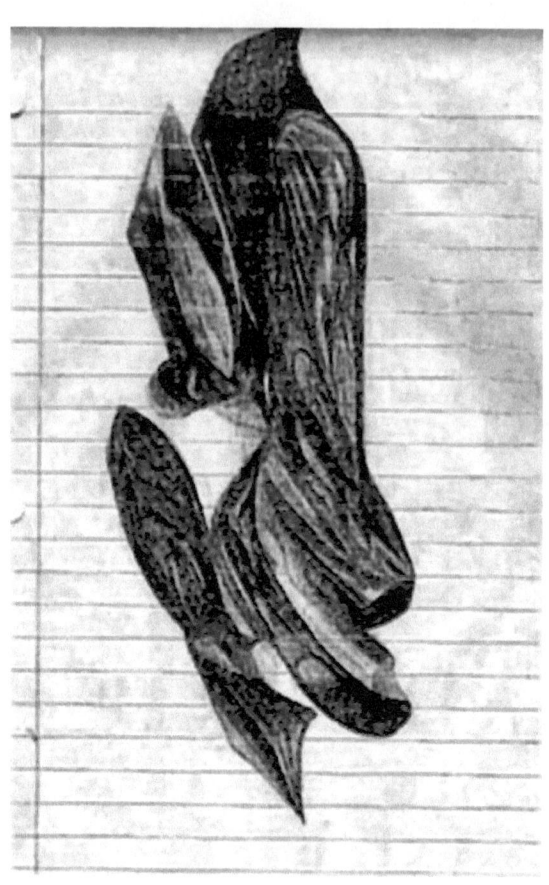

Vivid Slices

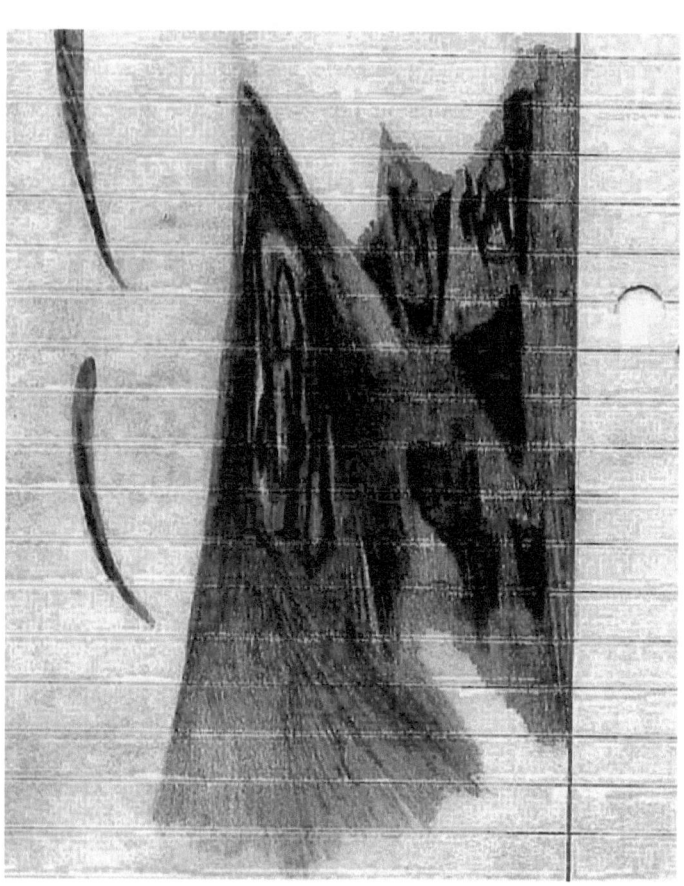

The Windows

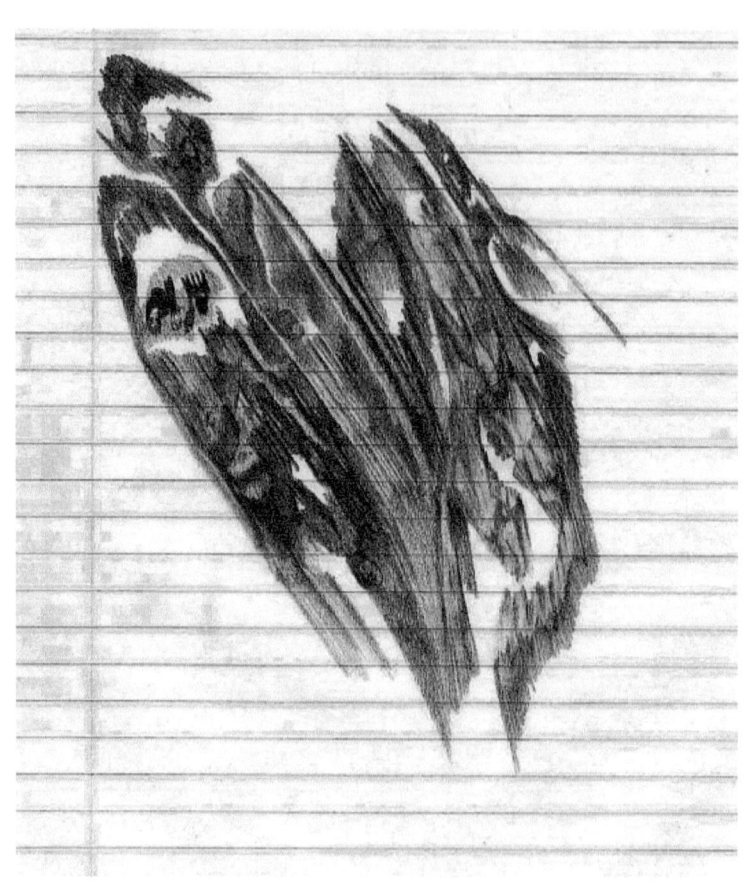

The Hermit

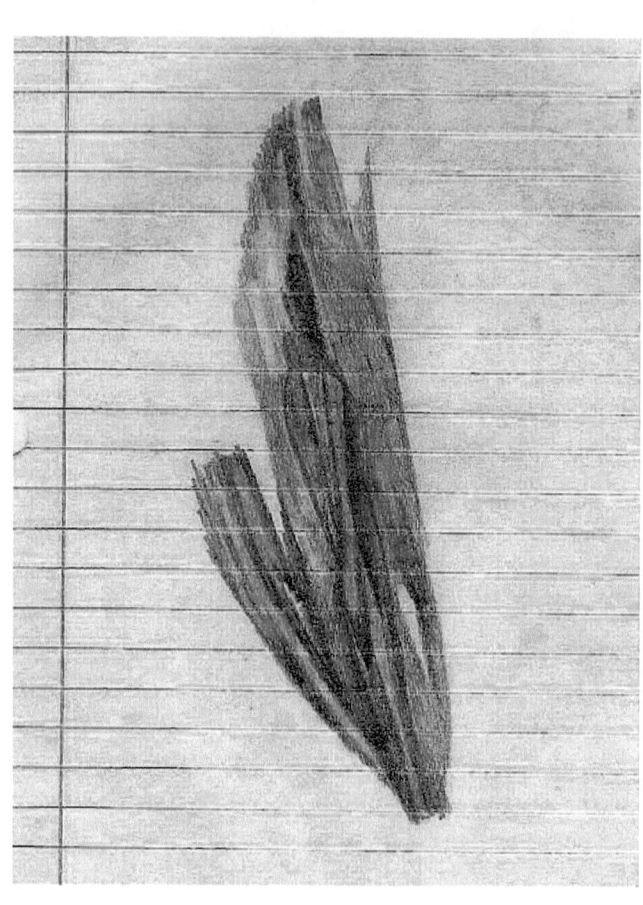

The Mistress of War

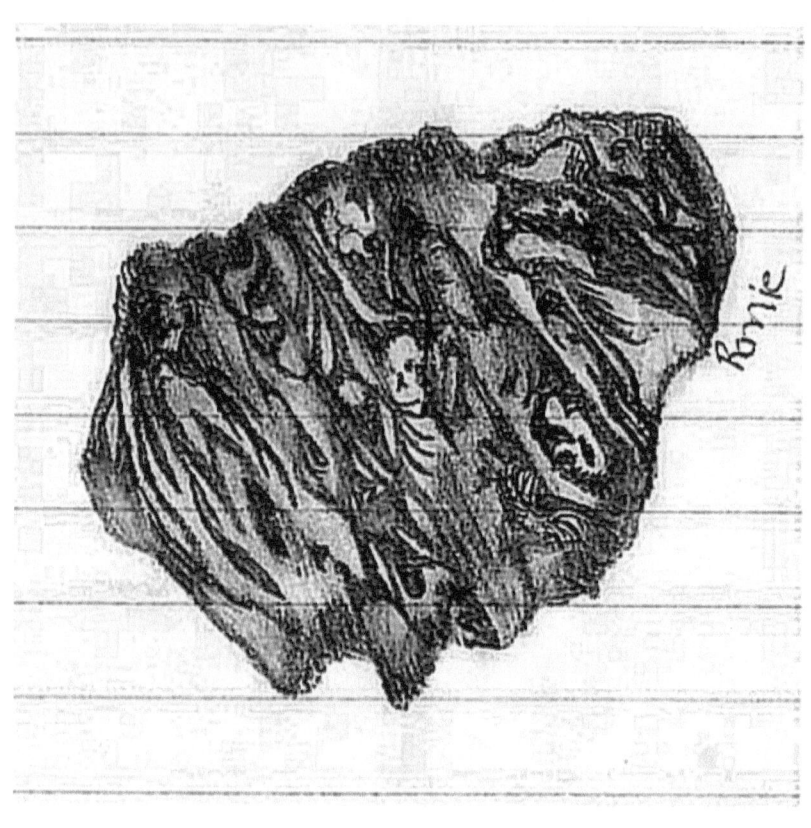

Ronie

Delusions

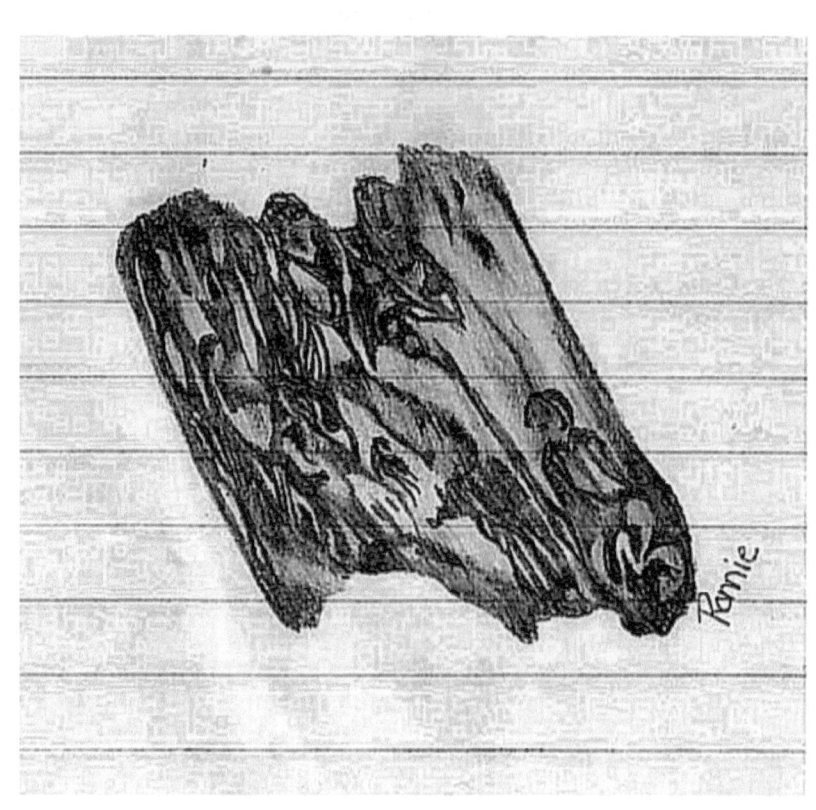

The Arcane

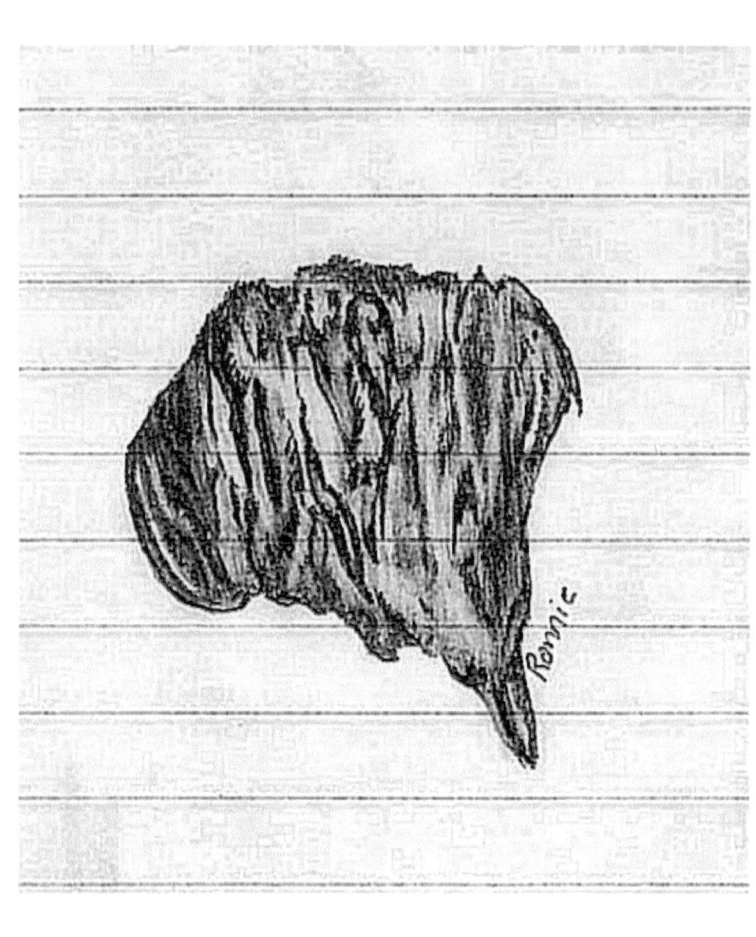

Secrets

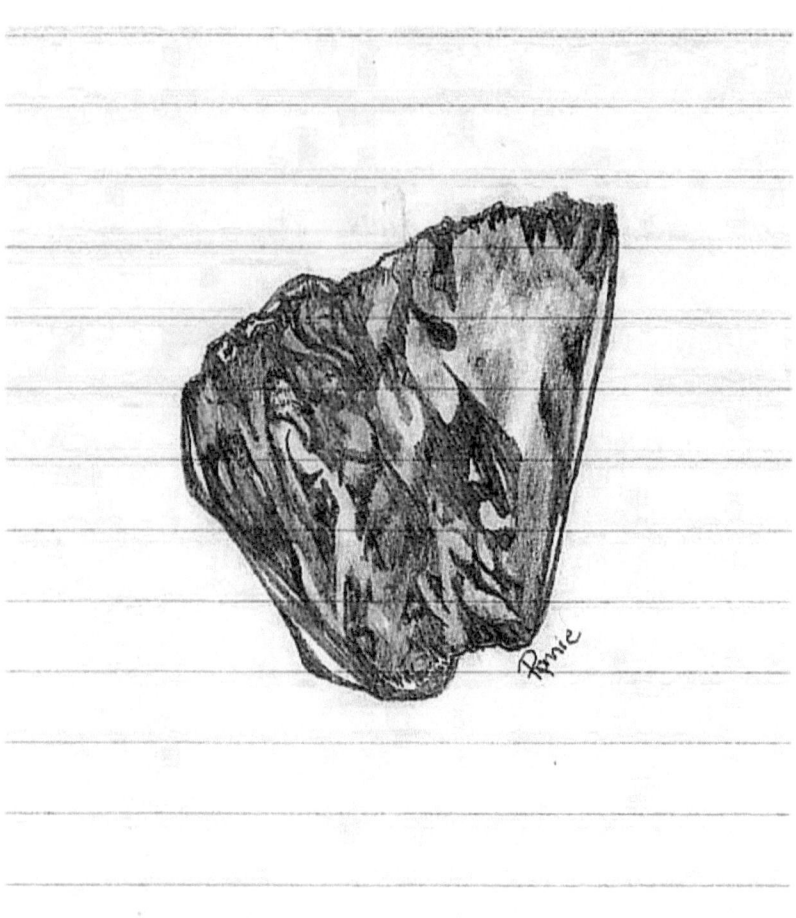

Faces in Shadow

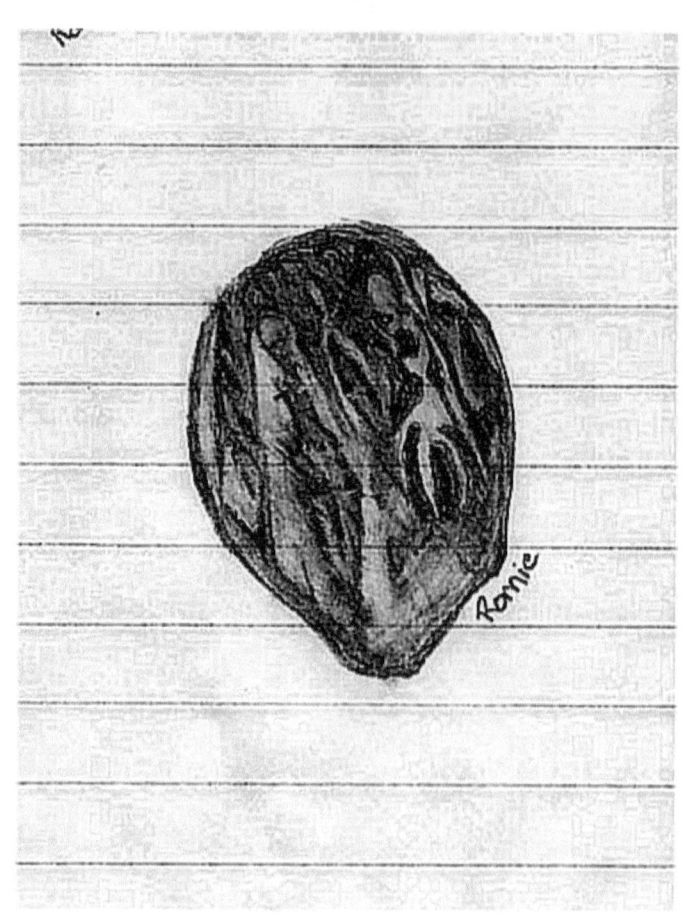

The Stare

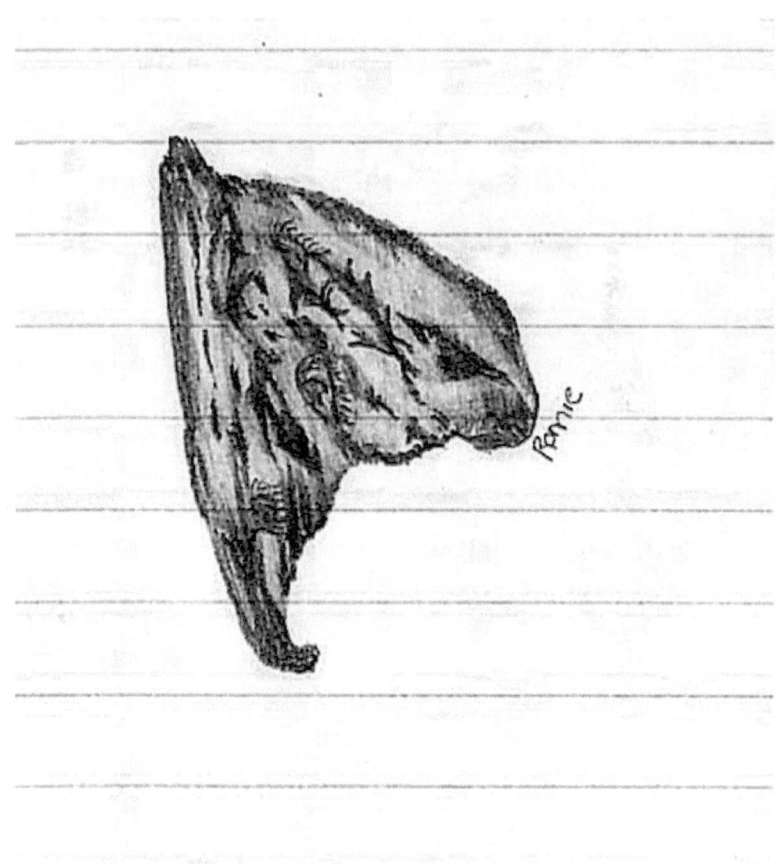

Man And Ghost

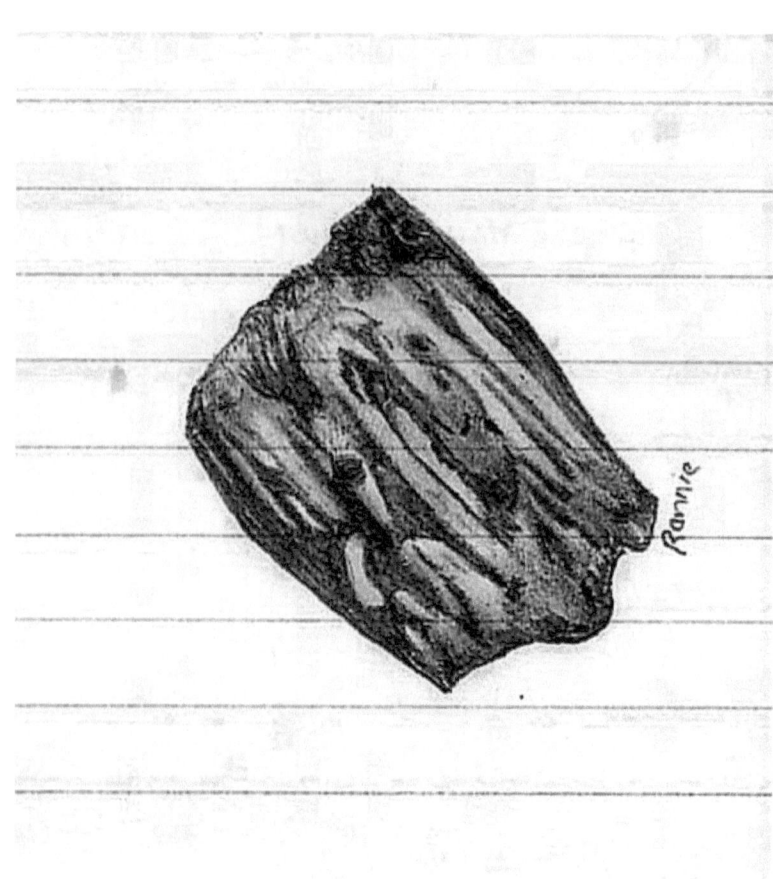

Clown Face

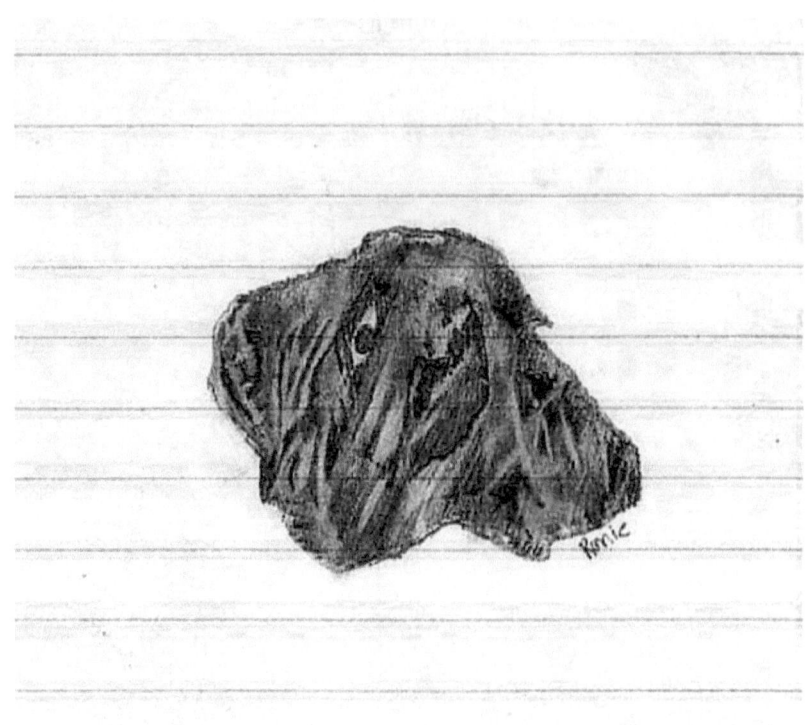

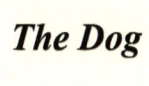

The Dog

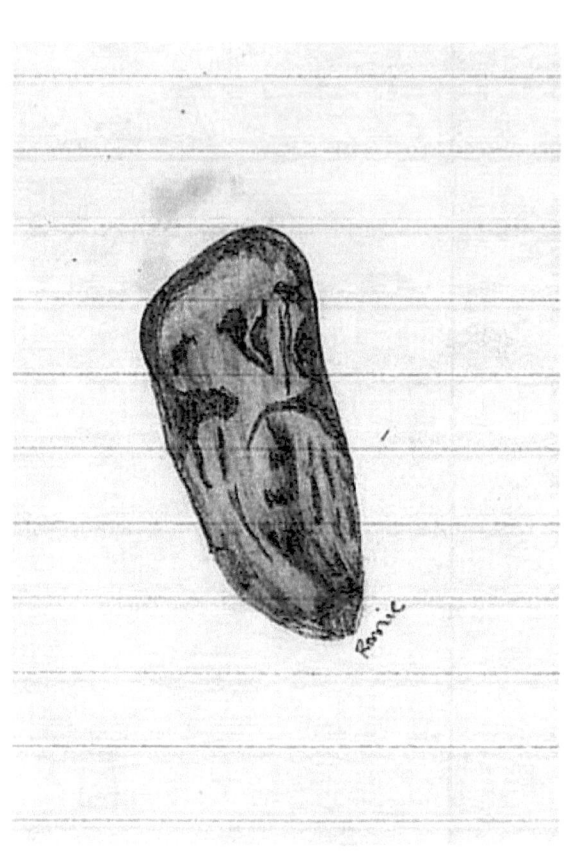

The Face

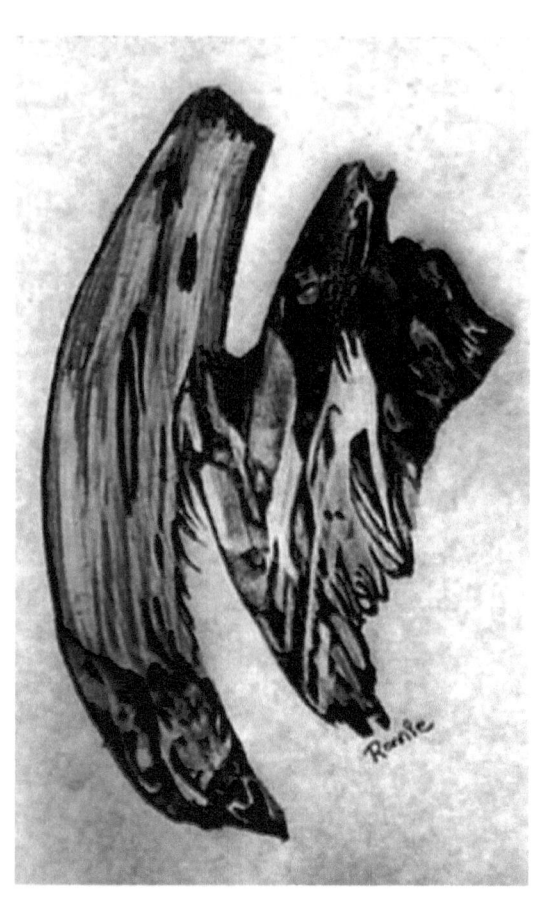

The Face

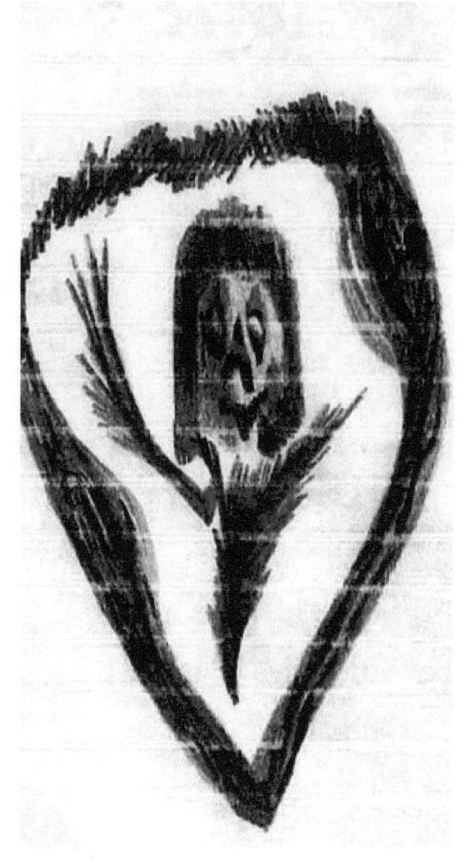

The Heart

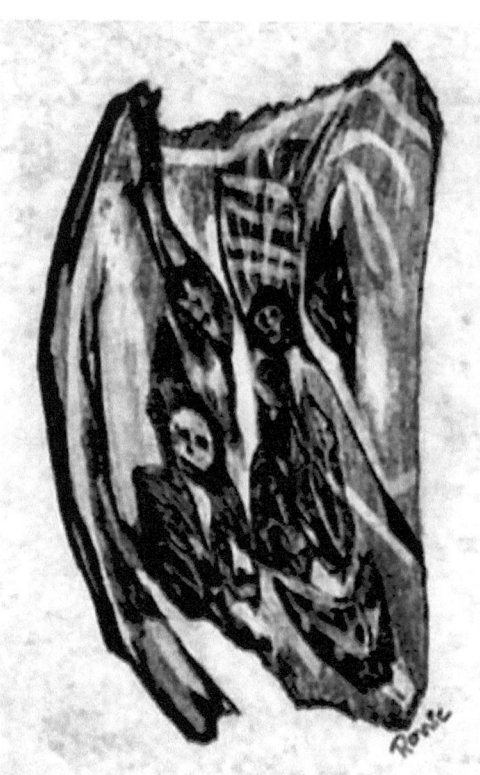

Shadows

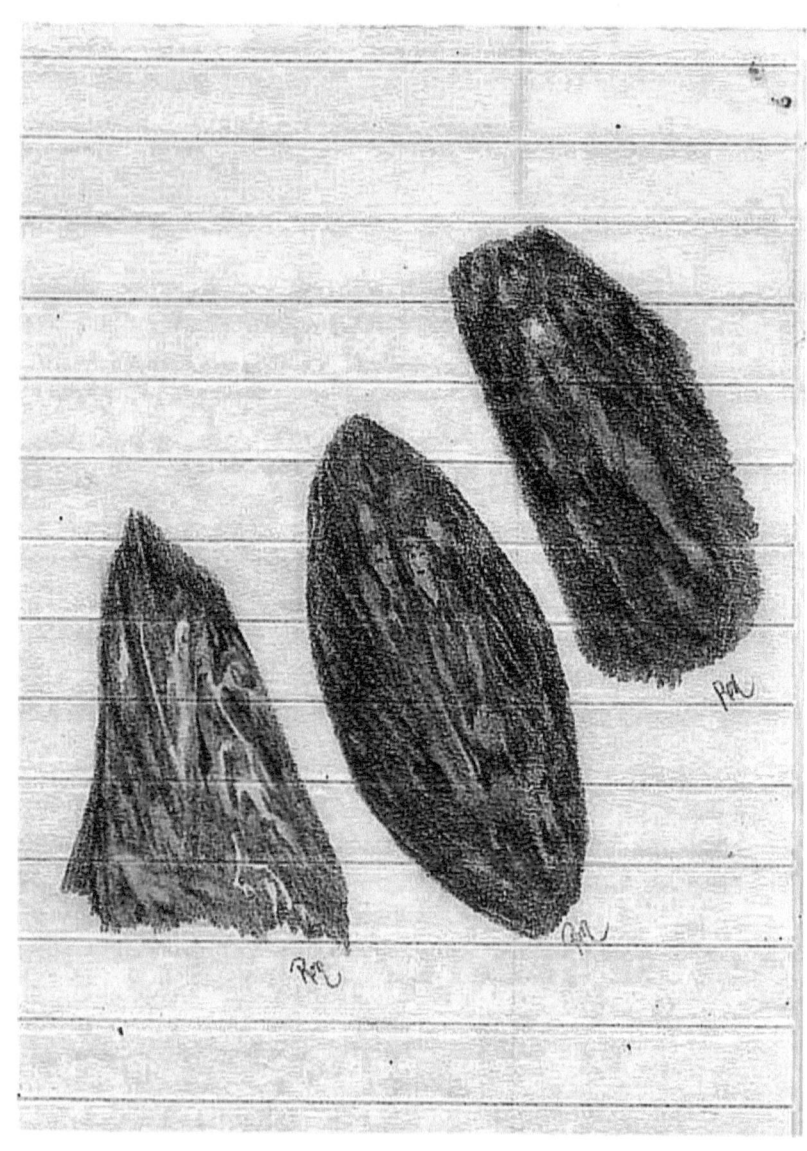

Three Maidens

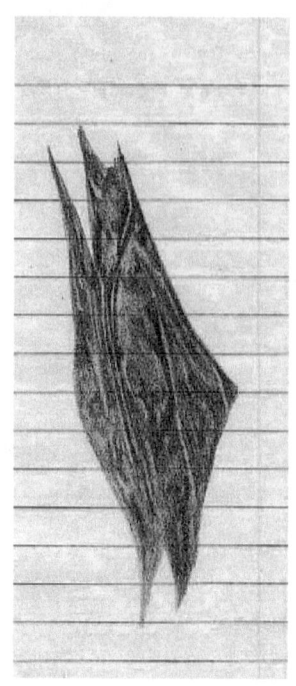

Surreal Secret

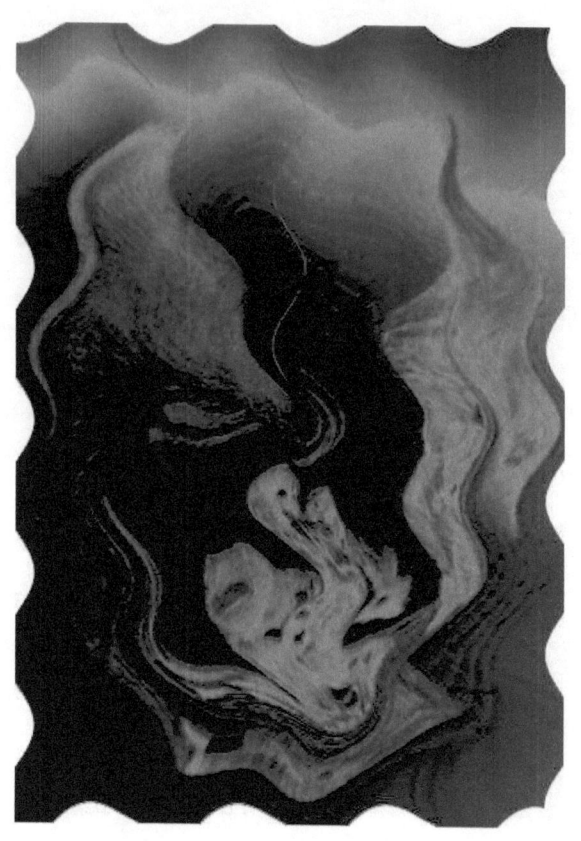

She Dreams

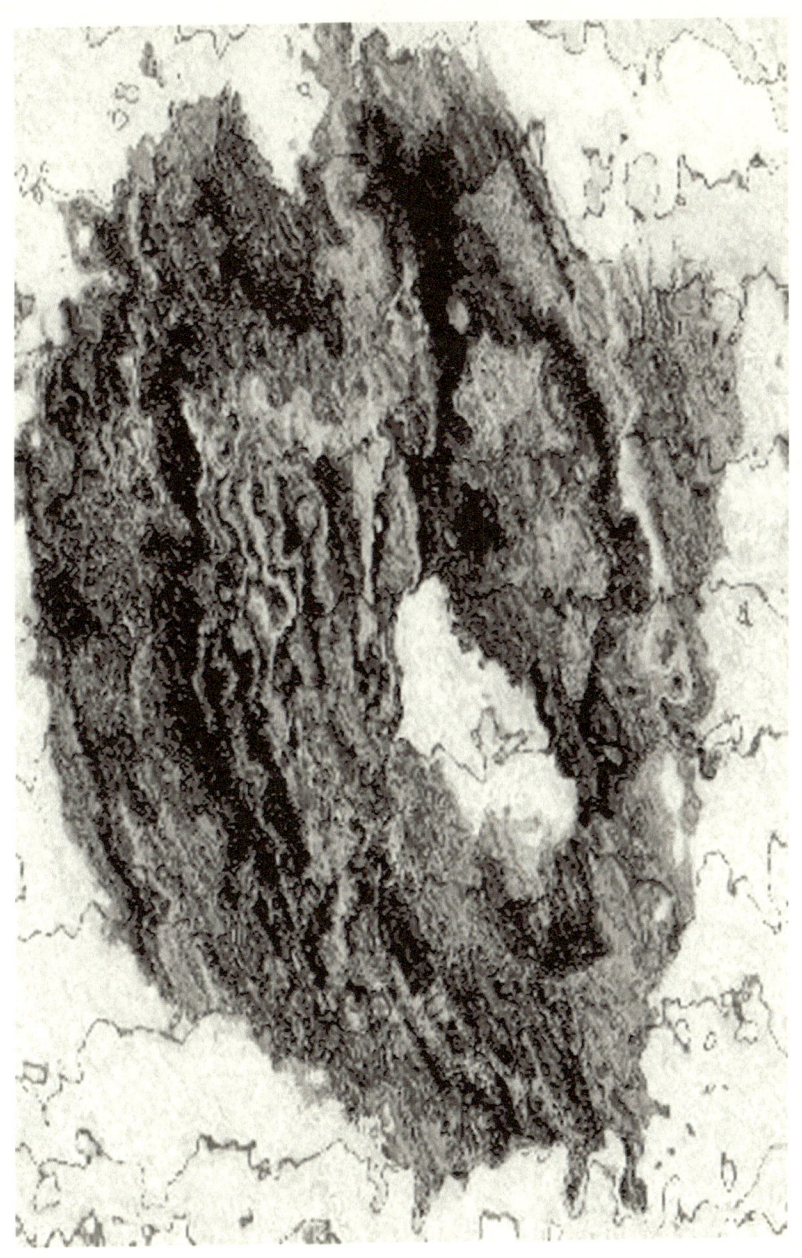

Prayers In Limbo

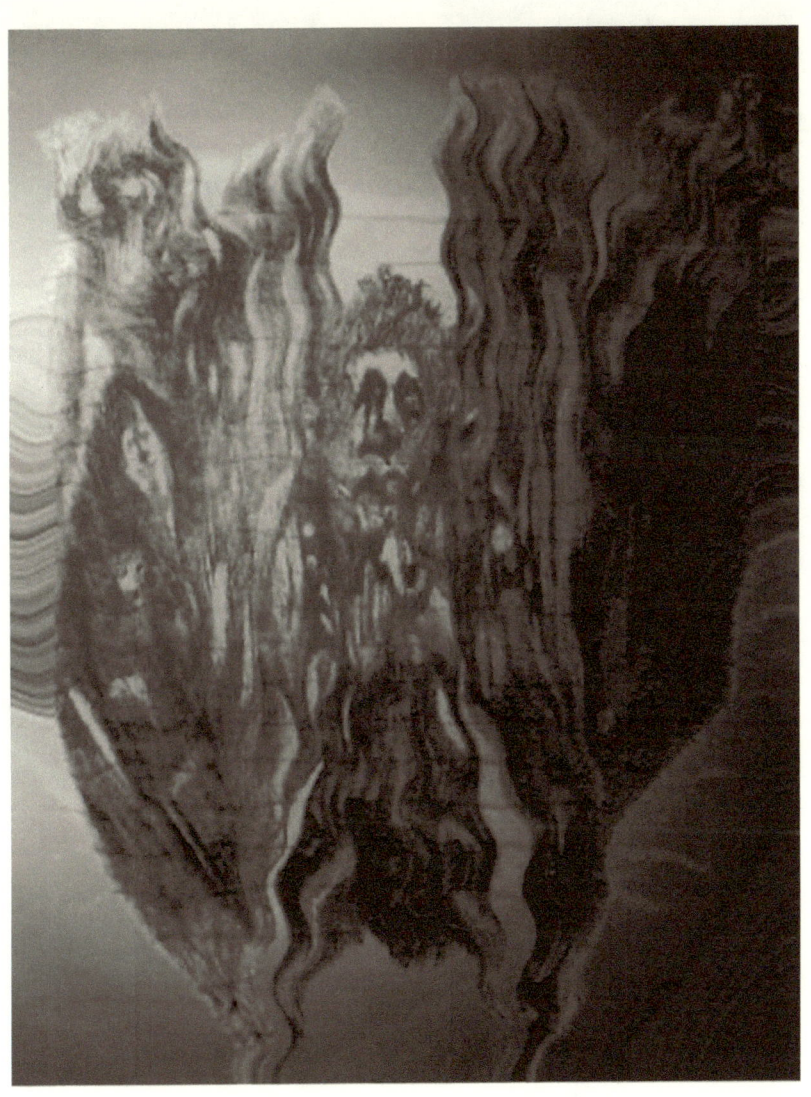

The Tears of A Butterfly In Sorrow

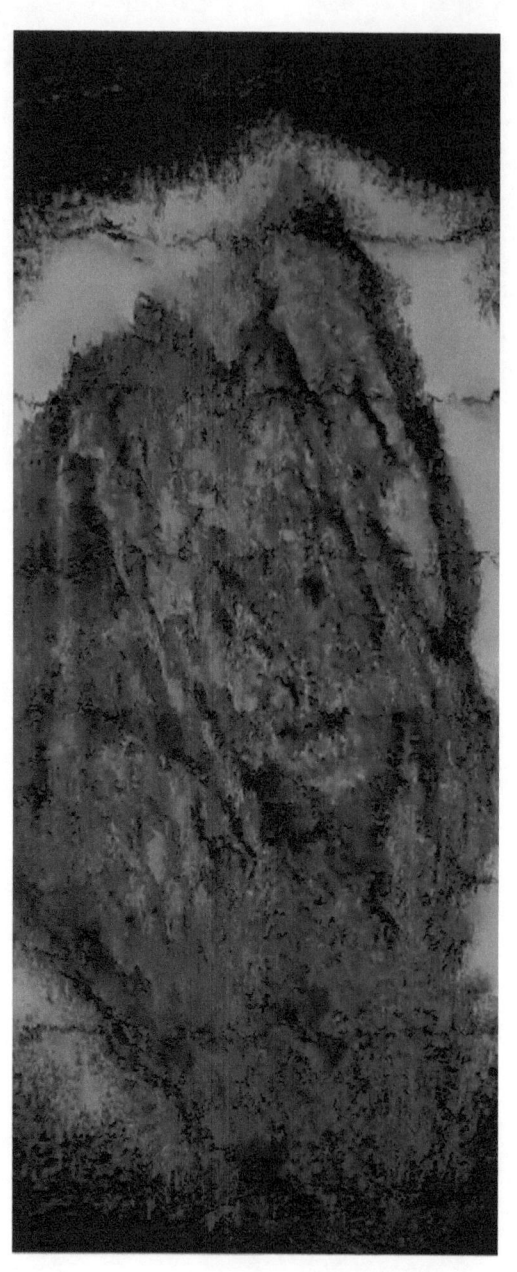

Escape to Avalon

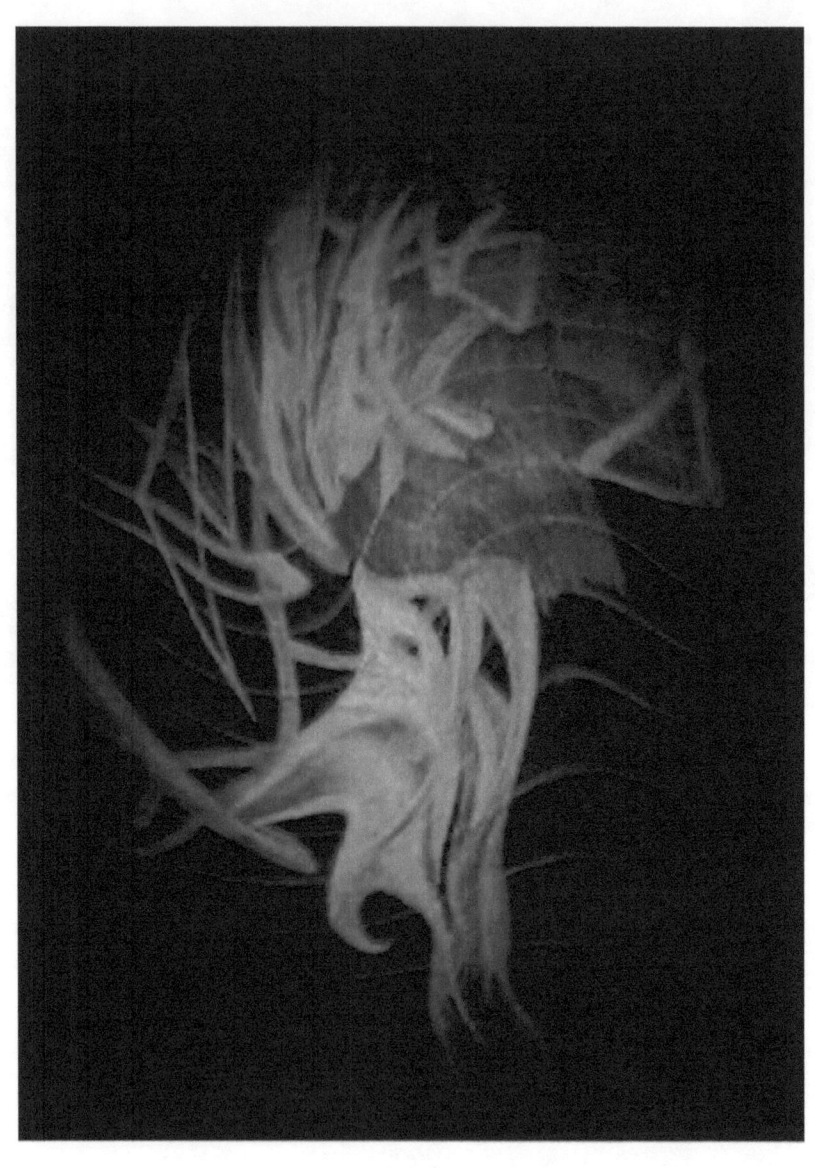

Angles In Red

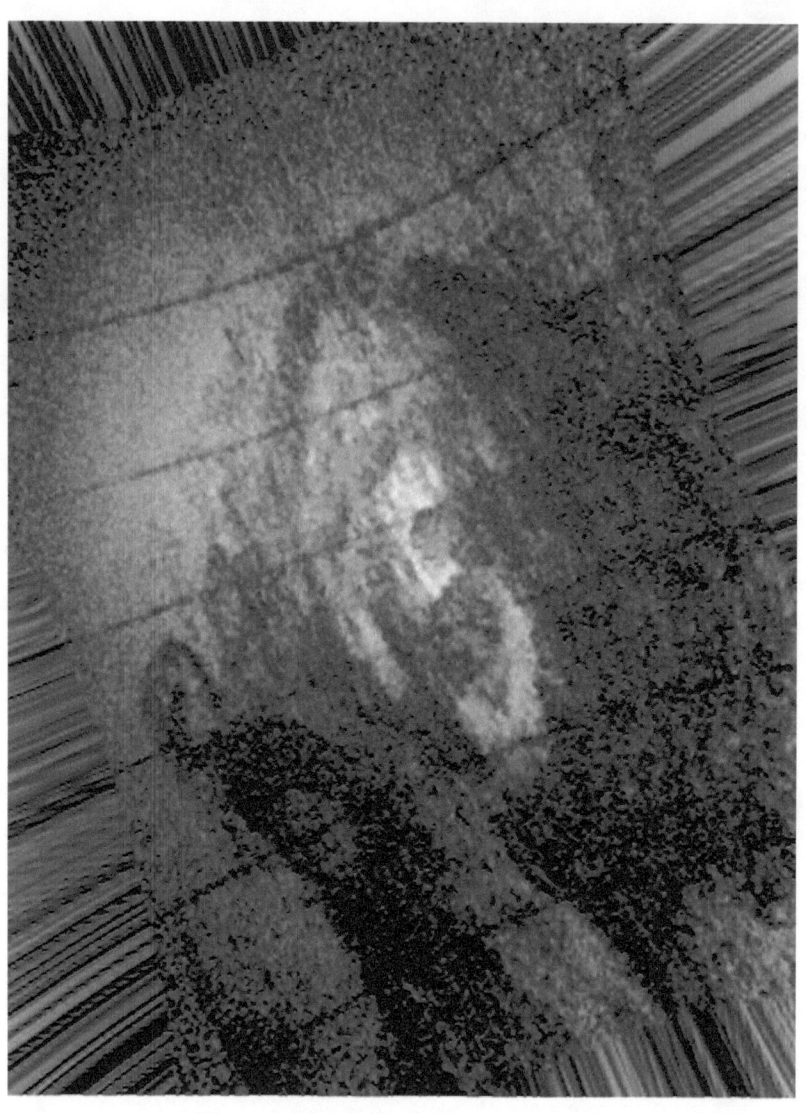

Woman In Misery and Contemplation

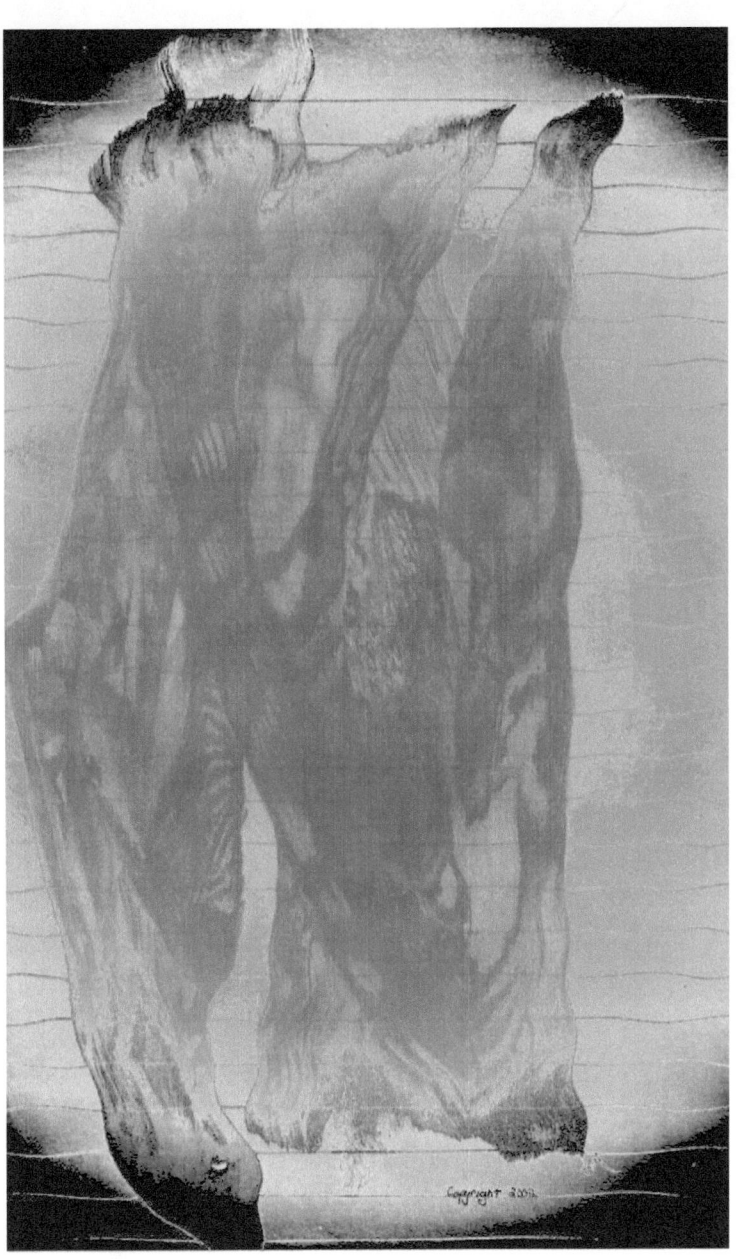

Butterfly 2

Thank you for your Attention!!!

Notes

Notes

Notes

Notes

Notes